SIMPLE PRAYER

DESTINY IMAGE BOOKS BY DRS. DENNIS AND JEN CLARK

Abiding in the Secret Place

An Ancient Blueprint for the Supernatural

Breaking Soul Ties

Flowing in the River of God's Will

A Practical Guide to Self-Deliverance

Releasing the Divine Healer Within

The Supernatural Power of Peace

Deep Relief Now: Free, Healed, and Whole

Live Free

Visit Drs. Dennis and Jen Clark online at www.forgive123.com.
Visit the online school directed by Jason Clark at http://training
.teamembassy.com.

Drs. Dennis
and Jen Clark

SIMPLE PRAYER

A GUIDED JOURNAL
TO QUIET YOUR SOUL,
CONNECT WITH GOD, &
ABIDE IN HIS PRESENCE

DESTINY IMAGE® PUBLISHERS, INC.

P.O. Box 310, Shippensburg, PA 17257-0310

"Publishing cutting-edge prophetic resources to supernaturally empower the body of Christ"

This book and all other Destiny Image and Destiny Image Fiction books are available at Christian bookstores and distributors worldwide.

For more information on foreign distributors, call 717-532-3040.

Reach us on the Internet: www.destinyimage.com.

ISBN 13 TP: 978-0-7684-7507-4
ISBN 13 eBook: 978-0-7684-7508-1

For Worldwide Distribution, Printed in the U.S.A.
1 2 3 4 5 6 7 8 / 27 26 25 24 23

CONTENTS

Preface

WELCOME TO THE *SIMPLE PRAYER GUIDED JOURNAL*

Congratulations on your commitment to measurably improve the quality of your emotional, spiritual, and physical life. We don't want you to feel alone on this journey.

Those who embark on this journey are truly a special breed—hungry for more of God and willing to pay the price of Christian discipline. You are the very person that God has been looking for. You, like Mary of Bethany, are choosing the better part that won't be taken away (Luke 10:38-42).

When I embarked on this quest with Dennis as my mentor, it was just the beginning of what has been the most exciting and fulfilling time of my life. I can hardly even remember the pains and fears that were once my constant companions. The fruit of this extraordinary transformation has manifested in an absence of internal and external conflict and a closer walk with God. I know that my story will become your story too.

Be sure to keep a written record of all the words and impressions that the Holy Spirit quickens in you. Enjoy the amazing quest that lies ahead.

Until I meet you in person,

DR. JEN CLARK

SECTION 1

DAYS 1-8

HONORING GOD AS A PERSON

GETTING STARTED

WHAT IS SIMPLE PRAYER?

Simple Prayer is one of several terms which are used to describe prayer in which a person waits quietly before the Lord. Perhaps the best word to describe Simple Prayer would be abiding. In John 15, Jesus tells us to abide in Him, and He gives us the metaphor of the vine and the branch. A branch must be connected to its life source, the vine, to be able to flourish and produce fruit.

> *Abide in Me, and I in you. As the branch cannot bear fruit of itself, unless it abides in the vine, neither can you, unless you abide in Me. "I am the vine, you are the branches. He who abides in Me, and I in him, bears much fruit; for without Me you can do nothing.... By this My Father is glorified, that you bear much fruit; so you will be My disciples* (John 15:4-5, 8).

ABIDING

As you wait silently, without speaking, simply become aware of the presence of the Lord in your heart. This way of prayer is both a relationship with God and a discipline which encourages growth of the relationship. *Simple Prayer* is not intended to replace other types of prayer. However, it does bring deeper meaning to all prayer and leads you from more active kinds of prayer into prayer in which you abide in God and commune with Him.

Surely I have calmed and quieted my soul, Like a weaned child with his mother; Like a weaned child is my soul within me (Psalm 131:2).

The Lord your God in your midst, The Mighty One, will save; He will rejoice over you with gladness, He will quiet you with His love, He will rejoice over you with singing (Zephaniah 3:17).

Our Spiritual Heart

When the Bible speaks about our spiritual heart, it is not referring to the chest area or physical heart. In the Old Testament and New Testament alike, words such as *belly* or *bowels* are regularly translated *heart* in English. In John 7:38 in the King James Version of the Bible, Jesus refers to the heart by the word *belly* in the Greek, *"He that believeth on me, as the scripture hath said, out of his* belly *shall flow rivers of living water."* The heart is the center of man's *inward life* and the sphere of *divine influence.*

The Bible tells us that the heart is below the chest, in the belly area, and is the seat of emotion. According to the Bible, the *emotional heart* is in the *belly.*

Door of the Heart

The door of the heart is the *will.* It is in the belly. Scripture tells us that the door of the heart can either open or shut, choose or refuse. Jesus says, in Revelation 3:20, *"Behold, I stand at the door and knock. If anyone hears My voice and opens the door, I will come in to him."*

The Bible tells us the belly or gut is not only the seat of our spirit and emotions, but also of our *conscience* and *will,* the faculties of choice and decision making. The word *will,* in some translations of the Old Testament, is translated *reins,* or literally our *kidneys.*

I the Lord search the heart, I try the reins [kidneys]*, even to give every man according to his ways, and according to the fruit of his doings* (Jeremiah 17:10 KJV).

God-Indwelt

When we are saved, we become God-indwelt. We welcome Jesus into our heart and His Spirit is joined with our spirit. *"But he who is joined to the Lord is one spirit with Him"* (1 Corinthians 6:17).

> *The kingdom of God is within you* (Luke 17:21).

The Secret Place

As we yield to the Lord within our heart, we are drawn into the secret place in our innermost being where we commune with Him. Instead of focusing on the thoughts in our head, we turn our focus to Jesus within. Yielding instantly connects us to Him spirit to Spirit. *"It is God who is at work in you, both to will and to work for His good pleasure"* (Philippians 2:13 NASB).

> *He who dwells in the secret place of the Most High Shall abide under the shadow of the Almighty. I will say of the Lord, "He is my refuge and my fortress; My God, in Him I will trust"* (Psalm 91:1-2).

PRACTICE

- Close your eyes and yield to Jesus within your heart. It is like relaxing, down low. It is the opposite of being tense.
- That opens the door of your heart in prayer.
- Jesus is the Prince of Peace.
- Sense the peace of His presence. (It is usually very subtle and gentle.)

The two necessary ingredients of abiding prayer are silence and stillness. If you have ever stilled your thoughts in your prayer time or church to quietly enjoy God's presence, you have already experienced silent prayer. The mind does not become blank, but awareness of God increases.

1. Silence
2. Stillness

"GOD-TOOLS"

We use our powerful GOD-TOOLS for smashing warped philosophies, tearing down barriers erected against the truth of God, fitting every loose thought and emotion and impulse into the structure of life shaped by Christ. Our tools are ready at hand for clearing the ground of every obstruction and building LIVES OF OBEDIENCE INTO MATURITY (2 Corinthians 10:4-5 MSG).

1. *God Tool Number One: Prayer*

Prayer is not talking, although it may include talking. Prayer is being with God, or communion with Him.

2. *God Tool Number Two: Forgiveness*

Forgiveness is the awesome gift that Jesus gave us to cleanse us of sin and remove walls separating us from God and other people. At the time of salvation all believers experience the initial glorious freedom and peace that forgiveness brings, but many believers don't understand how to continue to apply the God tool of forgiveness to deal with unresolved issues of the past or for practical help in daily life. Simple Prayer is designed to be your personal trainer to help you learn to live a forgiveness lifestyle.

BIBLICAL FORGIVENESS DEFINED

- Forgiveness must be from the heart, including thoughts, will and emotions

- Forgiveness is a Person. Christ is the Forgiver so He forgives through us.
- Forgiveness is not an option; it is a command.
- Forgiveness releases us so that our lives won't be poisoned.
- Forgiveness releases others so that God can work in their lives.
- Forgiveness is canceling a debt.
- Forgiveness is ceasing to sit in the place of judgment and releasing them to God, the Judge of the universe.

FORGIVENESS IS NOT:

- NOT releasing someone from their responsibility.
- NOT being a doormat.
- NOT pardon in the sense of removing consequences.
- NOT absolving another's sin.
- NOT just pretending to forget
- NOT reconciling with a person when boundaries still need to be established.

KEYS FOR HEALING PRAYER

- Christ is the Forgiver so forgiveness works every time!
- Forgiveness is instant, not a process.
- There is no "big or little." It is all easy for Jesus!
- Sequence is important, so always go in God's order.
- Pray through one thing at a time until you get peace.

GETTING STARTED

Decide to make the Lord your number one priority every day. You are making an appointment to meet with the King of the universe. You may want to set your alarm to awaken you earlier.

1. Decide on a time. If you don't devote a specific prayer time into your schedule it is too easy to skip.

   My devoted time is: _____

2. Choose a quiet place with a comfortable chair in which to sit.

   My quiet place is: _____

3. Get your Bible, a pen or pencil, and your journal so that you can keep a written record.

   ☐ Bible

   ☐ Pen

   ☐ Journal

4. How long should you spend in prayer? We suggest a minimum of 20 or 30 minutes at a time.

5. Try to pray through a cycle of at least 3 emotional healings per day.

6. If possible, ask someone to be your prayer / accountability partner.

   ...says the Lord, who created you.... and He who formed you... "Fear not, for I have redeemed you; I have called you by your name; you are Mine" (Isaiah 43:1).

THE SEVEN THRONES OF LIFE

During my journey I (Dennis) had an encounter with God that caused me to shift my attention from receiving love and attention from God, to making myself vulnerable to the Lord, so He could search my heart and adjust different aspects of my life.

Ordinarily, being scrutinized for things that needed adjustment would have been threatening for me. I now found myself willing to be vulnerable in the presence of the One I loved and trusted the most. Remember, even a corrective word from the Lord has all the love of heaven behind it! I was learning to trust Him because I now knew His great love for me.

In the weeks and months during which God was daily searching my heart, He asked me to present seven areas to Him and allow Him to "adjust" my attitudes and actions. I call them the "Seven Thrones" of life. I could sit on the throne, or let Jesus be Lord of each area.

> *Search me, O God, and know my heart; Try me and know my anxious thoughts; And see if there be any hurtful way in me, And lead me in the everlasting way* (Psalm 139:23-24 NASB 1995).

> *Who can understand his errors? Cleanse me from secret faults. Keep back Your servant also from presumptuous sins; Let them not have dominion over me. Then I shall be blameless, And I shall be innocent of great transgression* (Psalm 19:12-13).

SEVEN THRONES

Spirit

Our human spirit can be strengthened in our faith journey. In Ephesians 3:16, Paul prays that God would strengthen believers "*with might through His Spirit in the inner man.*" As we grow in the Lord, our spirit becomes stronger. Welcome the presence of God to flood your spirit and impart spiritual strength.

Mind

Welcome God to show you any unscriptural or ungodly thoughts that you need to deal with. He wants you to have the mind of Christ, not flesh or evil. If you have a thought that doesn't line up with the Bible, allow the

Lord to replace it with the truth. Repent of unkindness. Repent of thoughts of doubt or unbelief.

Will

I allowed the Lord to show me areas where I was trying to be in control and failing to trust Him. Is there any stubbornness or rebellion? Are you giving in to manipulation or striving in willpower? Release control back into the hands of God. God wanted me to be a Sabbath son and learn to rest in Him.

Emotions

All negative emotions, the loss of peace, indicate our relationship with the Lord has temporarily been interrupted. He doesn't leave us, but we can allow people and circumstances to disconnect us from communion with God. I learned that forgiveness or release (into God's hands) always restored the peace I felt in the presence of the Lord.

Body

Jesus lives within us as our Forgiver but He is also our Healer and Miracle Worker. I learned to welcome Jesus, who lives within my heart, into my physical body for health and healing.

Relationships

During this time of welcoming presence, I allowed the Lord to show me any issues or offenses I had in relationships with people. I discovered that He wanted me to live in supernatural peace without walls of separation.

Finances and All Possessions

Everything we have belongs to God. We are simply stewards of what the Lord has given us. I learned to hold money with a loose hand so I could sow when prompted by the Holy Spirit but also to inquire of God about financial decisions and purchases.

God has also given us time, material possessions, and gifts and talents. We are stewards who are accountable to God for how we use everything God has entrusted to us. Was I wasting time? Was I neglecting to care for my possessions (like changing the oil in the car and making necessary repairs on the house)? Was I developing and growing in my gifts or was I failing to use all the Lord had given to me?

As you invite the Holy Spirit into these areas of life, train yourself to be sensitive to any areas where you feel resistance to yielding. Allow Him to overcome your reluctance and fill those areas anyway. It is important to honor that sensitivity and respond in your relationship with God (2 Peter 3:18). Cultivate awareness of even subtle changes and distinctions.

> *Therefore gird up the loins of your mind [not passive], be sober, and rest your hope [open] fully upon the grace that is to be brought to you at the revelation of [Messiah] Jesus* (1 Peter 1:13).
>
> *[G]row in the grace and knowledge of our Lord and Savior* (2 Peter 3:18).

Simple Prayer

DAILY PRAYER

Set aside a devoted time of prayer daily. Get in an attitude of prayer and silently focus on Christ within, in your heart.

1. **HONOR:** Start by presenting yourself to the Lord in humility and adoration as His servant. Honor God as a real person who is right there with you, not far away. Yield to His presence and desire God's will, His thoughts (revelation), and His emotions (the fruit of the Spirit).

2. **AWARENESS** (Listen, feel, see): As you sense the presence of God, pay attention to the atmosphere. What facet of His nature is the Lord revealing to you. Love, comfort, peace, refreshing, holy anticipation? What words come to mind that describe the atmosphere? Pay attention to scriptures or pictures which corroborate what you feel. Don't just think about it, but receive, absorb, drink in. Allow it to be written on your heart. Later, take some action by writing it down, cherishing it, speaking of it, and living it!

3. **TIME:** How long should you spend in prayer? Enough time for your flesh to become still in the presence of God. How can you tell? Your thoughts will cease to wander, you will feel peace, and you will lose the urge to go do something other than pray (Psalm 131:2; Isaiah 40:31).

4. **LOVING FUNCTIONS:** Your human spirit cooperates with the Holy Spirit in:

a. *Receiving:* When you yield to Jesus, drink in or absorb the anointing.

b. *Forgiving:* Yield and let a river of forgiveness flow to others.

c. *Loving:* Let a river of love flow out from your heart.

d. *Releasing (people and circumstances):* From your gut, release people, worries, or circumstances into the hands of God until you feel peace.

e. *Resisting:* When you are focused on the secret place you will be guarded by supernatural peace. (From this place, you are shielded from the enemy.)

Simple Prayer

HEALING PRAYER

We do not have to tolerate carnal toxic emotions. When Jesus died on the cross, He carried away *"our griefs and carried our sorrows"* (Isaiah 53:4). Our emotions were originally created to be conduits of the fruit of the Spirit. In the Garden of Eden, before he sinned, Adam only experienced the love, joy, and peace of God—God emotions—in his emotions. Only after sin entered did Adam and Eve experience toxic emotions such as fear, guilt, anger, and shame.

> *But the fruit of the Spirit is love, joy, peace, longsuffering, gentleness, goodness, faith, meekness, temperance* (Galatians 5:22-23 KJV).

When Adam sinned, his spirit was separated from God. He died a spiritual death. Harmony between God and man was fractured. Adam became flesh-ruled instead of spirit-ruled. Man's fallen nature and God's heavenly nature no longer matched. Adam's thoughts, choices, and emotions—in his soul—were now carnal, ruled by flesh.

The fruit of the Spirit is *evidence* that the kingdom of God is at hand: *"For the kingdom of God is...righteousness and peace and joy in the Holy Spirit"* (Romans 14:17). When Jesus rules, righteousness, peace, and joy are *evidence* His kingdom has come. We know that peace and joy are emotional, but what about righteousness? It is emotional too, because righteousness may be defined as "the love of God in action." God is love and love is the source of everything done by God.

When we experience love, peace, and joy in our heart, therefore, we know we're operating out of the right kingdom: *"[T]he kingdom of God is within"* (Luke 17:21). The love chapter of the Bible, 1 Corinthians 13, describes how we should allow God's love to work through us: *"Love is patient, love is kind."* Paul writes in regard to the fruit of the Spirit: *"the fruit of the Spirit is love, joy, peace, patience, kindness, goodness, faithfulness, gentleness, self-control; against such things there is no law"* (Galatians 5:22-23 NASB).

Notice that the word "fruit" is singular. Love is *one fruit*. In Galatians 5:22-13, the love of God is described as one fruit with nine different expressions.

- One fruit: Love
- Joy is love rejoicing
- Peace is love ruling/resting
- Patience is love enduring
- Kindness is love caring
- Goodness is love motivating
- Faithfulness is love trusting
- Meekness is love esteeming

[I]n lowliness of mind let each esteem others better than himself (Philippians 1:3).

- Self-control is love restraining

[Love] does not demand its own way (1 Corinthians 13:5 NASB).

The love of Christ controls us (2 Corinthians 5:14 NASB).

EMOTIONS ARE SIGNALS

When a believer yields to God, they experience God emotions as the fruit of the spirit. When a Christian fails to yield, they experience carnal emotions. Your emotions sound an alarm to let you know which Kingdom is ruling.

When we feel the fruit of the Spirit, the Prince of Peace is ruling in our heart. *Negative emotions* mean that the enemy has taken some ground. How do you know if you have entered enemy territory? Negative emotions. How do you know if you are in God territory? God emotions, or the fruit of the Spirit!

> *The kingdom of God is...righteousness and peace and joy in the Holy Spirit* (Romans 14:17).

Forgiveness is the God-tool that rescues us out of enemy territory and takes us into God territory. God rescued you from the kingdom of darkness and granted you citizenship in the Kingdom of God. Forgiveness keeps you there. Any time we feel a negative emotion, forgiveness can wash it out and replace it with supernatural peace.

> *He* [God] *has delivered us from the power of darkness and conveyed us into the kingdom of the Son of His love* (Colossians 1:13).

> *He brought me to the banqueting house, and his banner over me was love* (Song of Songs 2:4 AMPC).

If you are a born-again believer, it doesn't mean you have lost your *salvation* when you temporarily get in enemy territory, any more than a United States citizen loses their citizenship if they visit a war zone in a foreign country. It just means that you need to get back into God territory so you will be safe!

JESUS THE FORGIVER

Jesus is the *Forgiver*. He went to the Cross to give the *gift of forgiveness* to mankind. Christ the Forgiver does the forgiving in and through us. Forgiveness is *grace* in action.

Through grace we are saved, and by grace we live in the Spirit. It is no longer I who *live*, but Christ who lives in me. Therefore, it is no longer

I who *love,* but Christ who loves in me. It is no longer I who *forgive,* but Christ who forgives in me!

> *My old self has been crucified with Christ. It is no longer I who live, but Christ lives in me. So I live in this earthly body by trusting in the Son of God, who loved me and gave himself for me* (Galatians 2:20 NLT).

RECEIVING SALVATION

Remember when you got saved? What happened when you prayed, "Jesus, I ask You to save me and forgive me for my sins"? You *opened* the door of your heart to Jesus and received *forgiveness instantly* as a free gift. You then experienced *peace* with God.

> *Behold, I stand at the door and knock. If anyone hears My voice and opens the door, I will come in* (Revelation 3:20).

> *In Him we have redemption through His blood, the forgiveness of sins* (Ephesians 1:7).

> *...there is peace with God through Jesus Christ* (Acts 10:36 NLT).

WALKING IN THE SPIRIT

How should you *live* the Christian life? You live the Christian life by walking in the Spirit. You can only "walk in the spirit" when your spirit connects with God's Spirit. In John 15, Jesus says, *"I am the vine, you are the branches. He who abides in Me, and I in him, bears much fruit; for without Me you can do nothing."*

A believer walks in the spirit by maintaining a spiritual connection with God or *abiding* in Him. As soon as we disconnect, we are in the flesh. In the book of Colossians, we learn that the way we received salvation is the pattern for our Christian walk.

As you therefore have received Christ Jesus the Lord, so walk [live] in Him (Colossians 2:6).

Because Jesus *is* our peace, when peace rules, He rules (see Eph. 2:14; Col. 3:15). Peace is evidence of the Lordship of Jesus. Therefore, peace is evidence that Jesus is Lord of our life at any given moment. When we sense His peace, He is on the throne of our life. When peace rules, we can be at rest and go about our daily life with the assurance that God is in control. If we lose our peace, we need to either deal with an attitude in our heart or make a course correction in our life to have peace again. It's that simple.

Having shod your feet with the preparation of the gospel of peace (Ephesians 6:15).

Forgive in Three Directions

GOD-SELF-OTHERS. Forgiveness goes in three directions: toward God, self, and others. Sometimes a person needs to forgive in two or more directions. If in doubt, forgive. You can't love or forgive too much!

1. *God:*

God didn't do anything wrong, but people get angry at Him anyway. Sometimes people feel hurt that God didn't do what they wanted Him to do, or become angry that God didn't *stop* something from happening. Forgiving God gets *your* heart right by releasing your judgments toward Him.

2. *Self:*

If you are angry, disappointed with, or ashamed of yourself, you need to *receive* forgiveness for judging yourself so harshly. Frequently people are much harder on themselves than other people! (When you receive forgiveness, drink it in from your gut.)

3. *Others:*

Release forgiveness to other people. When you forgive others, it sets *you* free!

HEALING PRAYER STEPS

> *PRAYER* —*Close your eyes and get in an attitude of prayer.*
>
> *FIRST*—*First person or situation. What is the first person or situation that comes to mind—picturing a person or memory of an event?*
>
> *FEEL*—*Feel the feeling. Allow yourself to feel. What is the emotion you feel in your gut?*
>
> *FORGIVE*—*Forgive. Yield to Christ the Forgiver within and allow a river of forgiveness to flow from the belly until the emotion changes to peace.*
>
> *FACT*—*Fact. After forgiving and getting peace, if there is a lie, renounce the lie out loud. Next, ask the Lord for the truth (scriptural fact) and receive it.*
>
> *FILL*—*Fill. (1) Forgive first, then (2) release demands on people to give you what you needed. (3) Receive filling from Christ within.*

Most of the time, we only need the steps of First, Feel, Forgive. In only one out of every 30-40 prayers do we need to deal with a lie (Fact) or be filled in the area of an emotional need (Fill).

Day One

God with You

I am the vine, you are the branches. He who abides in Me, and I in him, bears much fruit; for without Me you can do nothing (John 15:5).

...those who honor Me I will honor (1 Samuel 2:30).

Daily Prayer

Now you are ready to begin. Each day when you come into the presence God, start by honoring Him. Start by getting into an attitude of prayer. Close your eyes and place your hand on your belly area, your spirit man, to help you focus on Christ within your heart.

- Honor God as a real Person who is with you.
- Ignore distracting thoughts and just keep returning your focus to Christ within.
- If you think of something important that you need to remember later, make a note and return to prayer.
- Write down any impressions or scripture verses that come to mind.

_____

_____

_____

_____

_____

_____

_____

_____

_____

_____

_____

_____

_____

_____

_____

_____

_____

HEALING PRAYER

The Lord knows all about you and He wants to set you free from troubled areas hidden in your heart. Many times the conscious mind forgets all about hurts and fears but they still affect our lives even if they are under the surface.

- Allow the Lord to reveal anything He wants, allowing forgiveness to bring healing.

- Keep a brief record of what you pray about and what the Lord reveals to you.

- Pray in the order that things come to mind, and write down revelation that you get.

- During this challenge try to deal primarily with as much baggage from the past as you can.

- Try to pray through at least three issues every day.

Day Two

HARMONY WITH GOD

Do not be conformed to this world, but be transformed by the renewing of your mind [Gk. nous - mind, will, emotions], *that you may prove what is that good and acceptable and perfect will of God* (Romans 12:2).

For as the heavens are higher than the earth, so are My ways higher than your ways, and My thoughts than your thoughts (Isaiah 55:9).

DAILY PRAYER

"Lord, I want to touch You in prayer this morning. Knit my heart with Your heart in the reality of Your presence." You are a thinking, willing, feeling being and you were created by God to be in perfect harmony with Him—His thoughts, His choices, and His emotions.

- Prayer brings you into alignment with the heart of God, to change you.
- Allow the Lord to reveal His thoughts to your heart, adjust your choices, and unite you with His love.

_____

_____

_____

_____

_____

HEALING PRAYER

Deal with any issue(s) that comes to mind, even if you think it may seem small and insignificant. Come into the presence of the Lord just like a child who runs to the embrace of a loving parent.

- Invite the Lord to search your heart. Let forgiveness wash away pain.
- Write down a brief description of issues that come up, and note changes in perception after forgiveness.

_____

_____

_____

_____

_____

_____

_____

_____

_____

_____

_____

_____

_____

_____

_____

Day Three

CHRIST IN YOU

God willed to make known what are the riches of the glory of this mystery among the Gentiles: which is Christ in you, the hope of glory (Colossians 1:27).

DAILY PRAYER

Make room for God to rise up within you, over your mind, will, emotions. Many believers don't have a clear understanding about who they are in Christ and how very near He is. God dwells in heaven, but He also dwells in your heart. God is with you. His glory is within you. You do not have to beg Him for His presence, all you have to do is yield to Him.

_____

_____

_____

_____

_____

_____

_____

_____

_____

_____

_____

_____

HEALING PRAYER

You are coming to offer yourself to the Lord. He sees you as a New Creation, which is your real identity. God desires to reveal Himself to you and for you to glimpse the glorious treasure hid in your heart in Him. Cleansing and healing the heart remove barriers that prevent you from knowing Him more fully and from knowing who you really are in Christ.

- Enjoy God's love even in the process of sanctification.
- Allow the Lord to soften your heart and increase your sensitivity.
- Pray through a cycle of the people and situations that the Lord brings to mind.

Day Four

COMMUNION AND INTIMACY

The Spirit Himself bears witness with our spirit that we are children of God (Romans 8:16).

God is Spirit, and those who worship Him must worship in spirit and truth (John 4:24).

DAILY PRAYER

When we are born again our spirits can commune with God but the carnal mind, will, and emotions (soul) cannot know God. Because the fallen nature, the soul of man, is not at all like God's nature, we can commune with God only by the spirit. Therefore, man must quiet the soul and surrender to the Holy Spirit to be in communion with God. When you yield to the will to God, your spirit touches God, and the spirit takes authority over your soul. Yield to Christ within and welcome His presence to touch every area of your life. Welcome Him to strengthen you in your innermost being, to flow through your mind, will, and emotions.

_____

_____

_____

_____

_____

_____

_____

_____

_____

Healing Prayer

Do not become frustrated if something interferes with your prayer time, such as a phone call or doorbell ringing. Simply persevere and return to prayer as soon as you can. If you oversleep or feel upset with yourself, receive forgiveness. Your heavenly Father is delighted that you are drawing closer to Him. He does not expect perfection and neither should you.

- It brings pleasure to God's heart every time you set aside time to commune with Him.
- Do not fight runaway thoughts. Just ignore them while you keep returning your attention to Christ within.

Day Five

MAKING SPACE FOR GOD

We love Him because He first loved us (1 John 4:19).

He chose us in Him before the foundation of the world, that we should be holy and without blame before Him in love (Ephesians 1:4).

DAILY PRAYER

Enjoy God's presence whether or not anything "happens." Being with God is more important than anything else. Just love Him and receive His love. Jesus has been eager for you to come be with Him so He can offer you His love. When you give Him your time and wait before Him, you are making space for Him.

_____

_____

_____

_____

_____

_____

_____

_____

_____

_____

_____

_____

HEALING PRAYER

Present yourself to the Lord. *"Lord, cleanse me of anything interfering with our relationship!"*

- When you present your heart to the Lord, pray according to His order.
- God knows how everything is connected and how you should pray.
- Deal with as much baggage from the past as possible.

Day Six

DEALING WITH DISTRACTIONS

The grace of the Lord Jesus Christ, and the love of God, and the communion of the Holy Spirit be with you all (2 Corinthians 13:14).

DAILY PRAYER

In His presence is fullness of joy (Psalm 16:11). If you have difficulty with distracting thoughts or circumstances that interrupt your communion with the Lord, do not become frustrated with yourself. Write them down and simply melt back into God's presence. Rejoice in spite of everyday trials and the troublesome situations of life. When you continue to release it all back to the Lord, He will cause everything to turn out for good by His love and grace. This is really what trusting God is all about.

Healing Prayer

It helps you keep your focus on Christ within if you keep your hand on your belly as a reminder. *"Lord, You may go anywhere in my heart. You are welcome to go anywhere You want. I give You permission You to search my heart right now."*

- Remember to go in order. Do not skip or ignore issues.
- Pray through each memory one at a time until you get peace.
- As soon as you get peace go on to the next person or situation that comes to mind.
- When you have prayed through a "cycle" there will be a perception of completion, or sense of rest.

Day Seven

THE GOODNESS OF GOD

Men shall speak of the might of Your awesome acts, and I will declare Your greatness. They shall utter the memory of Your great goodness, and shall sing of Your righteousness. The LORD is gracious and full of compassion, slow to anger and great in mercy (Psalm 145:6-8).

DAILY PRAYER

Reflect on the goodness of God as you commune with Him. Focus on Christ in you. Notice that when you are aware of loving God you experience a sense of gratitude. This is true praise from the heart. As you continue yielding to God's love, often the sense of peace that you feel in His presence begins to change to joy. That is the joy of the Lord. You are being strengthened by the Holy Spirit (Isaiah 40:31).

HEALING PRAYER

You are coming to offer yourself fully to the Lord without analysis, restriction, or censoring. You are surrendering yourself to your Lord. He is more than willing and able to restore whatever was withheld or taken from you (Joel 2:25).

- Allow the Lord to show you areas where childish delight was stolen.
- Forgive, release demands, and then allow the Lord to fill those areas.

REVIEW OF WEEK ONE

PRAYER PARTNERS:

If you have not yet done so, you may want to ask someone (a friend or your spouse) to be your prayer partner for healing prayer. It is helpful to be mutually accountable. Be sure to keep it confidential! If you can't pray together in person, prayer over the phone can be very effective. Give one another permission to not name names or give details.

My prayer partner is

1. What are the main thoughts that the Lord has been speaking to your heart? List a few of them here.

_____

_____

_____

_____

_____

_____

_____

_____

2. Write one or two scriptures that have spoken to your heart. Why?

_____

_____

_____

_____

_____

_____

_____

_____

3. What difficulties have you overcome? Which area has been the most
    problematic for you this week?

    ▪ Mind
    ▪ Will
    ▪ Emotions

_____

_____

_____

_____

_____

_____

_____

_____

4. What theme(s) have you noticed in your emotional healings? For
    example, rejection, betrayals, disappointment, etc.

_____

_____

_____

_____

_____

_____

_____

5. What lies (if any) have been replaced by the truth? Make a list.

LIE	TRUTH

NOTES

Day Eight

LEARNING TO ABIDE

...abide in My love (John 15:9).

DAILY PRAYER

True fruitfulness comes only from intimacy. Too many believers rely on their own resourcefulness rather than inquiring of God and relying on His power to accomplish. The ultimate goal in honoring God is to learn to abide in Him, connected at the heart, Spirit to spirit, breath to breath.

Healing Prayer

Are there some areas of your life with which you are frustrated even though you have tried to change? If you have been unsuccessful in accomplishing something in your life and you are angry at yourself, then you have not been trusting the Lord to do the changing. Ask the Lord to show you the roots and let Him deal with it. Then God's life can flow through your life. A branch on a vine simply allows life to flow through it.

- Allow the Lord to soften your heart and increase your sensitivity.
- When the Lord shows you that you have an inner demand for something, release it back into His hands. Let it go. He wants to have first place in your life.

SECTION 2

DAYS 9-12

LISTENING (AWARENESS)

Day Nine

INCREASED SENSITIVITY

Then they brought little children to Him, that He might touch them (Mark 10:13).

You will seek Me and find Me, when you search for Me with all your heart (Jeremiah 29:13).

DAILY PRAYER

Learn greater sensitivity in prayer to encounter God in TOUCH. Pay attention to the whispers of the Spirit. When you come before the Lord in prayer, and become quiet, notice the atmosphere in the room where you are praying. How would you describe it? Does it feel peaceful, like an embrace, sweetly affectionate, or safe and secure? As you pay attention to the atmosphere, note any descriptive words that come to mind. Write them down.

_____

_____

_____

_____

_____

_____

_____

_____

_____

_____

_____

_____

_____

HEALING PRAYER

It is particularly important to deal with childhood issues about parents. Wounds from parents have a tremendous influence in forming the foundations of our lives. Often people will just see a parent's face, but it is vital to deal with the specific memories that come to the surface. When you have emotional overreactions during the day, ask the Lord to show you where that got started in your life so that the root can be removed.

- Ask the Lord to show you memories of your father.
- If you feel a wall of resistance, the wall is your will. Allow forgiveness to flow through and remove the wall. (A wall is a defense mechanism of self protection, based in fear.)
- If you forgive but still feel an ache inside (for love, attention, approval) then release demands on him to meet that need, and drink in the love of God to fill the hole.

Day Ten

ABSORB AND CHERISH

[Martha] *had a sister called Mary, who also sat at Jesus' feet and heard His word... "Mary has chosen that good part, which will not be taken away from her"* (Luke 10:39, 42).

If the Lord shows you something or you get a word or verse, write it down while never leaving the precious union in the Spirit. Hold that word close to your heart, cherish is as heavenly treasure of priceless value. Absorb it, hold it in the anointing. Allow it to grow. The Lord is your Master; you are the student. As long as you remain at His feet, He will continue to reveal Himself to you.

DAILY PRAYER

Does a scripture verse come to mind? As you wait silently, stay focused, and notice that the anointing increases while you stay focused on the verse. Write down any additional impressions or words, but do not let your attention wander from the Lord Himself. In other words, don't start analyze mentally or begin researching in books, dictionaries, or commentaries, but just enjoy Him.

HEALING PRAYER

Pray through issues concerning your mother. Allow the nurture of the Lord to fill in places that didn't receive the love that you needed as a child. Some wounds were just painful, but this type of healing restores the damaged foundations of our lives.

- The Lord says He will care for us and give us what we needed even if we were forsaken by mother and father.
- Once again, it is necessary to forgive, release demands, then receive filling.

Day Eleven

HEAVENLY TREASURE

But we have this treasure in earthen vessels, that the excellence of the power may be of God and not of us (2 Corinthians 4:7).

DAILY PRAYER

You are indwelt by God! The God of the universe has chosen to reside inside you. *In Him we live, and move, and have our being* (Acts 17:28). So what is left for you to do other than to rest as He works in you and through you? You were a pauper, and He has filled you with the riches of heaven. Allow gratitude to arise in your heart, that God has blessed you with a great inheritance. He has lifted you up and made you a joint-heir with His very own Son. Selah.

HEALING PRAYER

Pray through areas where you have felt disappointed in your life. You don't have to understand, but you must give up the internal demand for a do-over based on your own understanding.

- Forgive people, forgive God, forgive yourself, and release situations back into God's hands.
- Receive forgiveness for insisting that God answer to you, rather than you being a servant to Him.

Day Twelve

SHALOM, SHALOM

You will guard him and keep him in perfect and constant peace whose mind [both its inclination and its character] is stayed on You, because he commits himself to You, leans on You, and hopes confidently in You (Isaiah 26:3 AMP).

DAILY PRAYER

Position yourself in awareness, touching spirit to Spirit. Remain in the Presence of God until you experience His PEACE in your whole being —mind, will, emotions are quieted. You cannot trust God and be anxious or stressed at the same time. How do we trust God in everyday life? One Old Testament definition of *trust* is "to make someone your refuge." Prayer should not be something that you leave behind when you leave your prayer closet, prayer is a Person who is always with you. All you have to do is open your heart to Him and you are instantly trusting in Him. If you begin to feel anxious, yield to Him and His peace will immediately return.

_____

_____

_____

_____

_____

_____

HEALING PRAYER

While you are in prayer, ask the Lord to reveal any areas of your life which you need to surrender more completely to Him. Pray through these areas one at a time, releasing each into the hands of a loving, capable God. If you feel any internal resistance you may need to face any fears, or strings, that are attached. Do not be afraid to face your fears head on, and be bold to release right through concerns and worries. This is a work of the Cross, because you are choosing God over your fleshly insecurities.

- Ask the Lord to show you situations from your childhood that are interfering with your ability to trust God, and pray them through.
- When you have forgiven, released, and have peace ask the Lord to speak a scripture verse. Drink it in, and allow it to deepen while you stay there awhile and enjoy being with Him.

SECTION 3

DAYS 13-38

TIME

Day Thirteen

DEEPER STILL

Deep calls unto deep at the noise of Your waterfalls; All Your waves and billows have gone over me. The LORD will command His lovingkindness in the daytime, and in the night His song shall be with me—A prayer to the God of my life (Psalm 42:7-8).

DAILY PRAYER

We recommend spending at least 20 to 30 minutes in prayer. Others suggest a minimum of 20 minutes *twice a day*. Let the Lord lead you and show you how He wants you to schedule time with Him. Allow yourself to stay a little longer in your time of prayer today. Quietness has settled...allow deep tranquility to envelope your heart, and let the Holy Spirit take you deeper still.

HEALING PRAYER

Welcome the Lord to go into every area of your life, past, present, and future. As you give Him time, allow His presence to saturate your heart.

- Ask the Lord to show you any areas in which He wants you to surrender more fully to Him.
- Release these areas to Him and notice how your awareness of His presence increases.

Day Fourteen

Yielding Increases Peace

Surely I have calmed and quieted my soul, like a weaned child with his mother; Like a weaned child is my soul within me (Psalm 131:2).

Daily Prayer

Enjoy where you are now, then practice yielding even more, and you will notice that the peace increases. Quietness has settled. Allow deep tranquility to envelope your heart, and let the Holy Spirit take you deeper still.

- If you feel any impressions or increase in God's presence, pay attention to how it feels in the atmosphere, and write down any words that come to mind, such as comforting, sweet, tender, and so forth.
- The impressions you sense are the whispers of the Spirit.

HEALING PRAYER

Welcome the Lord to go into every area of your life, past, present, and future. As you give Him time, allow His presence to saturate your heart.

- Welcome the Lord into all areas of your life and heart. If you feel resistance anywhere, simply agree with Him, yield, and He will melt away barriers.
- Every time a barrier is removed, your sensitivity increases.

Review of Week Two

1. What are the main thoughts the Lord has been speaking to your heart?

_____
_____
_____
_____
_____
_____
_____
_____

2. What impressions have you noticed in the atmosphere?

_____
_____
_____
_____
_____
_____
_____
_____

3. Write one or two of the scriptures that stand out. Why?

_____
_____
_____
_____
_____
_____
_____

4. What theme(s) have you noticed in your emotional healings this past week?

_____

_____

_____

_____

_____

_____

_____

5. Have you been practicing staying in peace in your daily activities? When you lose your peace, deal with it quickly through forgiveness and/or release and you will quickly return to peace. NOTE: This is the main thing that you should practice in everyday life during the Challenge.

_____

_____

_____

_____

_____

_____

_____

_____

6. Don't expect perfection or become disappointed in yourself. Rejoice in every baby step of progress!

_____

_____

_____

THOUGHT FOR THE WEEK

What counts is whether we have been transformed into a new creation. May God's peace and mercy be upon all who live by this principle; they are the new people of God (Galatians 6:15-16 NLT).

Only the Lord can bring transformation. You are being transformed into your New Creation identity, the real you. Each area of your life that is touched by God increases your anointing. An increased anointing allows you to release more of God to others.

Day Fifteen

GOD-PROTECTED

God's peace [shall be yours, that tranquil state of a soul assured of its salvation through Christ, and so fearing nothing from God and being content with its earthly lot of whatever sort that is, that peace] which transcends all understanding shall garrison and mount guard over your hearts and minds in Christ Jesus (Philippians 4:7 AMP).

DAILY PRAYER

Enjoy the sweet touch of God's Spirit not only in you, but as this touching increases, you feel God's PEACE guarding (garrisoning as a fortress) your heart and mind through Christ Jesus. Notice that your heart feels tranquil, and thoughts do not distract you or cause you to lose your peace.

HEALING PRAYER

Welcome the Lord to deal with hidden root areas that are connected to any current loss of peace showing up with the people and circumstances of your daily life.

- Pray through at least one complete cycle.
- Don't dismiss anything that comes to mind as trivial or unimportant, but go ahead and deal with it.

Day Sixteen

SURROUNDED BY GOD

I will say of the LORD, "He is my refuge and my fortress; My God, in Him I will trust." He shall cover you with His feathers, and under His wings you shall take refuge; His truth shall be your shield and buckler (Psalm 91:2, 4).

The heavens and earth will shake; but the LORD will be a shelter for His people (Joel 3:16).

DAILY PRAYER

Experience God touching you within as well as being encompassed all about by His Presence—a canopy of God's Presence. God Himself is your shelter, your armor, your protection.

- The enemy can't touch the fruit of the Spirit. As long as you are in peace, you are surrounded with God's protection.
- Allow God to teach you to wear the full armor of God, and walk in shoes of peace (Ephesians 6:15).

_____

_____

_____

_____

HEALING PRAYER

Allow the Lord to show you areas where you feel insecure and release them back into the hands of God. Fear and anxiety rob you of the ability to feel safe and secure in God.

- Invite God to search your heart for roots of fear.
- Perfect love casts out fear.

_____

_____

_____

_____

_____

_____

_____

_____

_____

_____

_____

_____

_____

_____

_____

_____

_____

Day Seventeen

SATURATED BY GOD

To know the love of Christ which surpasses knowledge, that you may be filled up to all the fullness of God (Ephesians 3:19 NASB).

DAILY PRAYER

Experience God filling and saturating your entire being with His goodness. Welcome Him into every fiber of your being spirit, soul, and body. Invite the Holy Spirit to touch and strengthen your spirit and flow through your thoughts, choices, and emotions. Welcome the Lord into all areas of your life, including finances and relationships. Finally, welcome His healing anointing into your physical body.

Healing Prayer

Your mind, will, and emotions are like the sails of a sailboat. When the wind blows and the sails are set properly, the wind moves the vessel. There is always a wind of some sort filling your sails, but it is either the wind of flesh or the Holy Spirit. Welcome the wind of God into your thoughts and allow Him to deal with unscriptural thinking. Invite Him into your choices to realign you with His will, and into your emotions to experience His peace.

- Allow God to deal with the roots of negative thoughts, choices, and emotional pain.
- Present yourself and your life back to God, as a love offering to Him.

Day Eighteen

MANTLE OF GOD'S LOVE

My people will live in peaceful dwelling places, in secure homes, in undisturbed places of rest (Isaiah 32:18).

Yes, I have loved you with an everlasting love; Therefore with lovingkindness I have drawn you (Jeremiah 31:3).

DAILY PRAYER

Feel PEACE deepening and the weight surrounding and covering you - a mantle of God's love wrapping around you. Rest in Him as you cherish and absorb His love for you. Welcome the love of God.

Healing Prayer

Cleansing and healing the heart remove barriers that prevent you from knowing God's love more completely. God loved you even before the foundations of the earth were formed. He loved you and carried you in His heart for æons and æons of time in eternity past. God loved you before you could ever love Him back or do anything to try to earn His approval. Don't work for His love, just accept it and allow Him to embrace you.

- Enjoy the love of God even in the process of sanctification. His love for you makes transformation possible.
- God knows where He is taking you and how to get you there, and He never expects you to be perfect. He can even fix your mistakes.
- Receive forgiveness for yourself and melt into His love.

Day Nineteen

STILLNESS

And behold, the Lord passed by, and a great and strong wind rent the mountains and broke in pieces the rocks before the Lord, but the Lord was not in the wind; and after the wind an earthquake, but the Lord was not in the earthquake; And after the earthquake a fire, but the Lord was not in the fire; and after the fire [a sound of gentle stillness and] a still, small voice (1 Kings 19:11-12 AMP).

DAILY PRAYER

Come into the presence of God today and wait with a quiet and expectant heart. As you wait quietly and wait before the Lord, allow the sense of communion with Him to grow and increase. Experience stillness within and stillness without. You are now drawing from another kind of life, a heavenly life source, with a heavenly language that can only be heard in gentle stillness, a still small voice.

HEALING PRAYER

Healing prayer removes obstacles in your life so that you can continue to bring the sense of that higher life into the mundane activities of daily living. Anything that robs you of your peace during the day can instantly be removed by forgiveness.

- Any root issues revealed and dealt with in your time of healing prayer will allow God to fill more of your heart.
- As God fills more of your heart, you will notice an increase in the peace of His presence all day long.

Day Twenty

STRENGTHENED BY GOD

Those who wait on the LORD shall renew their strength; They shall mount up with wings like eagles, they shall run and not be weary, they shall walk and not faint (Isaiah 40:31).

DAILY PRAYER

Whenever your spirit encounters God, you receive spiritual strength from Him. Sense the security, safety, and all sufficiency that comes from Him.

HEALING PRAYER

Welcome the Lord to search all areas of your life, past, present, and future. As He heals your heart, allow His strength to fill you.

- Pray through roots of weakness and failure in your life.
- Forgive God, self, and others.
- Release yourself from over responsibility, and place yourself in God's hands.
- Exchange your feeble ability and receive God's power.

Day Twenty-One

THE ALL-SUFFICIENT GOD

How precious is Your lovingkindness, O God! And the children of men take refuge in the shadow of Your wings. They drink their fill of the abundance of Your house; and You give them to drink of the river of Your delights. For with You is the fountain of life; In Your light we see light (Psalm 36:7-9 NASB).

DAILY PRAYER

God is a God of abundance, all powerful, and all-sufficient. Allow God to show you His goodness to you in the past. All God really wants is children who love Him and appreciate His lovingkindness. Notice you feel gratitude when you focus on the mercy and blessings of God.

- Practice loving and appreciating the Lord during daily activities.

_____

_____

_____

_____

_____

_____

_____

_____

HEALING PRAYER

Ask God to reveal areas where your own roots, mental strongholds, or attitudes have blocked the flow of blessing and provision that God wants to release in your life.

- Welcome the Lord to search your heart. Allow Him to remove barriers and cleanse attitudes.
- Every time a barrier is removed, you receive clarity and you can see doors of opportunity more easily.

REVIEW OF WEEK THREE

1. What has the Lord has been speaking to you during the past week?

_____

_____

_____

_____

_____

_____

_____

_____

_____

_____

2. In which areas of weakness did you welcome an exchange of God's strength?

_____

_____

_____

_____

_____

_____

_____

_____

_____

_____

_____

3. How has the love of God touched your heart this week?

_____
_____
_____
_____
_____
_____
_____
_____
_____
_____
_____

4. What theme(s) have you noticed in your emotional healings?

_____
_____
_____
_____
_____
_____
_____
_____
_____
_____
_____
_____

5. What lies (if any) have been replace by the truth? Make a list.

LIE	TRUTH

THOUGHT FOR THE WEEK

Lord Jesus, Your very nearness brings great peace within, and Your loving gaze, speaking of grace so infinite, fills my soul with joy and thankfulness. —CHRISTIAN GREGOR, 1723-1801

The only bliss which we possess on earth is loving God and knowing that He loves us. —CURÉ D'ARS, 1786-1859

Day Twenty-Two

GOD'S POWER IN YOU

It is God who is at work in you, both to will and to work for His good pleasure (Philippians 2:13).

DAILY PRAYER

The anointing working in you is God's power to perform. You were created by God to co-labor with Him. Yield to the power of God working within you.

Healing Prayer

You not only have Christ the Forgiver living in you. He is also your Healer, Miracle Worker, Resurrection and the Life—in YOU! Any hindrance to His power is on our part, not His. What is your need? Emotional healing? Physical healing? Just be sure not to set a time limit, but know that whenever you yield to His power, change is happening in you even if you can't tell any difference right at the time.

- Ask the Lord to remove any barriers in you, and welcome His power.

Day Twenty-Three

GOD'S PLEASURE

Blessed (happy, fortunate, to be envied) is the man whose strength is in You, in whose heart are the highways to Zion. Passing through the Valley of Weeping (Baca), they make it a place of springs; the early rain also fills [the pools] with blessing (Psalm 84:5-7 AMP).

The LORD takes pleasure in His people (Psalm 149:4).

DAILY PRAYER

Whenever you yield to God in prayer, you are actually touching the essence of heaven and are then able to emanate that atmosphere on earth. God takes pleasure in His people, blesses them, and releases them to bring blessing to others.

HEALING PRAYER

Christ the Intercessor lives in you. And He wants to flow through you to touch others to bring healing, comfort, and salvation.

- Seek the Lord to remove any barriers in you that quench the anointing flowing through you to touch others.

Day Twenty-Four

GOD'S STRENGTH

I cling to you; your strong right hand holds me securely (Psalm 63:8 NLT).

DAILY PRAYER

Abandon yourself completely into God's strength; be sure that He will uphold you. He is called Immanuel, or God with us, so you are never without help and you are never alone. God knows your weaknesses and is well acquainted with all your ways. He knows when you are facing dangers and trials, and He is already prepared to deliver you out of trouble.

HEALING PRAYER

Everyone has times of suffering in this life, but hidden roots are often the source of unnecessary trials and tribulation. Ask the Lord to search deep within your heart to remove the secret snares that trip you up.

- Invite the Lord to go anywhere He wants to bring you deliverance from bitter roots.

- If the Holy Spirit brings up an area of generational sin, feel the feeling, receive forgiveness for yourself, release forgiveness to any perpetrators, and release forgiveness back through the family line.

Day Twenty-Five

GOD'S LOVING CARE

*For the LORD God is a sun and shield; the LORD will give grace
and glory; No good thing will He withhold from those who walk
uprightly. O LORD of hosts, blessed is the man who trusts in You!*
(Psalm 84:11-12).

DAILY PRAYER

Consider the great privilege you have in knowing that God is caring for you
personally. Allow the Lord to bring to mind some of the many ways that He
has been there for you when you needed Him, how He has watched over
you, and provided for you.

HEALING PRAYER

Invite the Lord to search all areas of your life. Let go of the burdens that you have been carrying unnecessarily and welcome the tender care of the Lord. As He heals your heart, allow God to comfort you.

- Pray through roots of insecurity and fear in your life.
- Release disappointments into God's hands.

Day Twenty-Six

DIVINE INTIMATE CONTACT

Lean on, trust in, and be confident in the Lord with all your heart and mind and do not rely on your own insight or understanding. In all your ways know, recognize, and acknowledge [through divine intimate contact] Him, and He will direct and make straight and plain your paths (Proverbs 3:5-6 AMP).

DAILY PRAYER

Notice the word *acknowledge* in Proverbs 3:5-6. This does not mean to simply *think about* God, it means to maintain a spirit to Spirit connection with Him. Feel the richness of the awareness of Christ in you. Acknowledge that He is near you and available for you whenever you need Him. As you become aware of His presence, yield even more, and welcome the increased intimacy that comes by making this Spirit-to-spirit connection with God.

Healing Prayer

God has a good future planned for you and when you let the peace of God rule, He will guide you through any difficulties. You will be led by Him during times of uncertainty.

- God knows what lies ahead in your life. He is preparing you and ministering to you so that you will be ready. He knows how to orchestrate all situations.
- Receive forgiveness for impatience or insecurity and melt into His love.

Day Twenty-Seven

FOCUSED ON GOD

He who dwells in the secret place of the Most High shall abide under the shadow of the Almighty (Psalm 91:1).

DAILY PRAYER

Keep your entire being focused on Christ within. Welcome the presence of God saturating your entire being with His goodness. The Lord longs for you to learn to abide in Him every moment of every day. When you maintain your peace you have continual communion with the Lord. He has been searching for the one who will become a resting place for Him.

HEALING PRAYER

When you are disappointed with yourself run to the Lord and not from Him. Come to the Lord in humility because of your great need, but not with condemnation.

- Think of yourself as a small child who comes running to your loving Father God.
- Receive forgiveness as a free gift that you do not have to earn. You merely receive it with gratitude.

Day Twenty-Eight

ATTENTION INCREASES AWARENESS

But let it be the inward adorning and beauty of the hidden person of the heart, with the incorruptible and unfading charm of a gentle and peaceful spirit, which [is not anxious or wrought up, but] is very precious in the sight of God (1 Peter 3:4 AMPC).

DAILY PRAYER

Be increasingly aware of every nuance, every shift, every subtle change. When you pay attention to the whispers of the Spirit, your ability to sense nuances and flavors increases. Notice that the anointing increases according to your focus. When you turn your gaze inward toward your Bridegroom King, it is precious to Him. He calls you His beloved, and draws closer to you whenever you turn to Him.

HEALING PRAYER

Ask the Lord for boldness to allow Him to go into dark places in your heart that you have been unconsciously avoiding. Receive forgiveness for any anxiety and know that there is great freedom on the other side of facing your fear.

- Ask the Lord to show you anything that is hindering or interfering with your ability to hear His voice.
- Receive forgiveness and allow forgiveness to flow through walls.

REVIEW OF WEEK FOUR

1. What has the Lord revealed to you this week?

_____

_____

_____

_____

_____

_____

_____

_____

_____

3. How did the Lord bring further healing to your heart? Was there a particular pattern or theme that you noticed?

_____

_____

_____

_____

_____

_____

_____

_____

2. Remember how the Lord has been there for you, even when you didn't know that He was delighting in you, watching over you, and providing for you. The children of Israel struggled with lack of faith about God's tender care, and sometimes we do, too. Take a few minutes to remember the blessings of God.

I will bless you with a future filled with hope - a future of success, not of suffering. You will turn back to me and ask for help, and I will answer your prayers. You will worship me with all your heart, and I will be with you (Jeremiah 29:10-13 CEV).

FAITHFULNESS IN THE PAST	PRESENT TRIALS	FUTURE
1.	1. Look back to see how God moved on your behalf in the past.	1. God has good plans for you.
2.		2. Hope keeps you open to God's plans.
3.	2. He will help you overcome the trials of today.	
4.		
5.	3. God has already planned His best for your future!	
6.		

NOTES

_____

_____

_____

_____

_____

_____

_____

_____

_____

_____

_____

_____

_____

Day Twenty-Nine

YIELD TO THE WILL OF GOD

You...are controlled not by the sinful nature but by the Spirit, if the Spirit of God lives in you. And if anyone does not have the Spirit of Christ, he does not belong to Christ. But if Christ is in you, your body is dead because of sin, yet your spirit is alive because of righteousness. And if the Spirit of him who raised Jesus from the dead is living in you, he who raised Christ from the dead will also give life to your mortal bodies through his Spirit, who lives in you (Romans 8:9-11 NIV).

DAILY PRAYER

Yield your will to the will of God. When you touch Christ in you, His life becomes your life source. This is eternal life, zoë, that comes from God Himself, and it draws you inward into a heavenly realm far beyond mere natural life. A dear saint who lived in the late 19th through the early 20th centuries had lungs which were almost destroyed by disease. Her doctors said there was no conceivable way for her to still be alive. Yet she lived for a full forty years following that grim prognosis by continuously yielding to the God life within her.

_____

_____

_____

_____

_____

HEALING PRAYER

Ask the Lord to show you issues that are hindering you from drawing closer to Him.

- Pray through a cycle and write down revelation that you receive from the Lord.
- Allow forgiveness to flow through any walls of self-protection.

_____

_____

_____

_____

_____

_____

_____

_____

_____

_____

_____

_____

_____

_____

Day Thirty

ROMANCE OF WILLS

I delight to do thy will, O my God (Psalm 40:8 KJV).

If any man desires to do His will (God's pleasure), *he will know* (have the needed illumination to recognize, and can tell for himself (John 7:17 AMP).

DAILY PRAYER

Every time we dedicate our will to God in whatever happens to us, the union of love takes place. –Basilea Schlink, 1904-2001

Encounter this *Romance of Wills*—God's love, your choice. Yield more fully to the flow of God's will. God's will contains all that is His very best and most perfect plan for your life. Every moment contains a gift of God's love for you if you will receive it by yielding to Him. When you insist on maintaining your peace in each circumstance of life, you receive grace, and God will cause it to work for your good and His pleasure.

HEALING PRAYER

Invite the Lord to show you likes or dislikes that are interfering with your ability to join your will together with God's will. If there is any desire in your heart for any person, place or thing and you cannot be neutral about it, there is an unmet inner need from childhood behind it.

- Ask the Lord to show you where that got started in your life.

- Forgive whoever didn't meet that need, release demands on them. and then invite the Lord to fill the hole in your heart.

- When you feel peace, go to the Lord and present your desire before Him.

- If you are truly neutral, you can be at peace so God can say either yes or no, and choose His best for you.

Day Thirty-One

A Surrendered Heart

Keep and guard your heart with all vigilance and above all that you guard, for out of it flow the springs of life (Proverbs 4:23 AMP).

Daily Prayer

Think of your heart as a castle with high walls and the will is the door of access. As soon as you open the door in prayer you connect with Christ within. Opening the heart to the Lord in prayer time is much easier than learning to keep the door open all day long. That takes practice, and we have the opportunity to do this by learning the peace walk as a lifestyle (Ephesians 6:15). Emotions are your friends, because they tell you whether or not you are abiding in God.

Healing Prayer

Ask the Lord to show you any hidden roots that are connected to daily events which are causing you to lose your peace.

- Allow the Lord to bring to mind people or circumstances that cause you to overreact.
- Ask the Holy Spirit to show you where that reaction got started in your life.
- Forgive God, self, and others.

Day Thirty-Two

THE ALABASTER BOX

Then Mary took a pound of very costly oil of spikenard, anointed the feet of Jesus, and wiped His feet with her hair. And the house was filled with the fragrance of the oil. But one of His disciples, Judas Iscariot, Simon's son, who would betray Him, said, "Why was this fragrant oil not sold for three hundred denarii and given to the poor?" This he said, not that he cared for the poor, but because he was a thief, and had the money box; and he used to take what was put in it. But Jesus said, "Let her alone; she has kept this for the day of My burial (John 12:3-7).

DAILY PRAYER

Yield from the place of total surrender to Christ in you. Dedicate your life, an alabaster box filled with precious perfume, to the Lord in a deeper consecration. Allow love and gratitude to flow out of your heart to your Bridegroom King. It is a fragrance which delights His heart. It is a fragrance that you can release into the atmosphere around you all day long.

HEALING PRAYER

Present your heart to the Lord and allow Him to search your heart, with the request that He may have any areas not yet fully surrendered to Him.

- Pray through root issues by forgiving and releasing areas back to God.
- Invite the Lord to soften any areas where you have hardness of heart.

Day Thirty-Three

TOTAL SURRENDER

This hope is a strong and trustworthy anchor for our souls. It leads us through the curtain into God's inner sanctuary (Hebrews 6:19 NLT).

DAILY PRAYER

Hope is synonymous with open. When a Christian has an open heart, they are emotionally open to God, other people, and life. Any loss of hope means that you have closed your heart and given up on God. Other people? Possibilities for good in life? Sometimes people give up because they have desires and demands that are not surrendered to God (see Day Thirty). Sometimes people shut down because they feel that they have received a promise from God, but they have waited so long, that they have stopped believing that God will bring it to pass. However, those who live a blessed life are OPEN to God's thoughts, God's emotions (the Fruit of the Spirit), and God's will and ways.

_____

_____

_____

_____

_____

_____

_____

_____

_____

_____

HEALING PRAYER

If you have been feeling hopeless, that is not from God. The only people who are hopeless are the unsaved who are the only ones who are "without Christ, being aliens from the commonwealth of Israel and strangers from the covenants of promise, having no hope and without God in the world" (Ephesians 2:12).

- Allow the Lord to show you any areas of bitterness or hopelessness.
- Forgive God, self, and others and release disappointments and expectations back into the hands of God.

Day Thirty-Four

RECEIVING

What you're after is truth from the inside out. Enter me, then; conceive a new, true life. Soak me in your laundry and I'll come out clean, scrub me and I'll have a snow white life... give me a clean bill of health. God, make a fresh start in me, shape a Genesis week from the chaos of my life (Psalm 51:6,7,10 MSG).

DAILY PRAYER

David wrote Psalm 51 in a time of deep repentance. Come before the Lord and ask Him to birth in you a newly intensified hunger for a new start. This is not the time to grow weary or be sidetracked, but allow the Lord to increase your dedication in pursuing more of Him through completing this Simple Prayer 60 Day Challenge. It is time to experience deeper depths in God. Write down any impression, scripture, vision while staying connected to God and taking each revelation inward presenting to God at the altar of your heart.

HEALING PRAYER

Grace is the personal presence of Christ in you, empowering you to be all that He called you to be and do all that He called you to do! When God touches the heart, He leaves a permanent deposit of His divine nature and increased anointing. Everything that God gives you, you can release to bless others.

- Welcome the Lord to show you areas where repentance is needed and then melt into His love to receive grace for change.
- If you see a pattern of repeated failure in that area, it is attached to some root area that is chaining you to the law of sin and death. Forgiveness breaks the chain.

Day Thirty-Five

FOCUS AND TRANSFORMATION

[D]o not be conformed to this world, but be transformed by the renewing of your mind [Gk. "nous" - thoughts, will, and emotions], that you may prove what is that good and acceptable and perfect will of God (Romans 12:2).

DAILY PRAYER

The Lord wants to bring you into perfect harmony with Him. Romans 12:2 has usually been taught to encourage believers to deal with the thought life, and that this practice alone would bring transformation. However, the word *mind* in the Greek is *nous*, which actually means the total being that includes *thoughts, will, and emotions*. This means that all three elements must be renewed for a believer to be transformed.

Healing Prayer

As you focus on Christ within this allows the Spirit to penetrate the depths of the heart.

- Allow the light of the Lord to search your heart for any patterns of thinking, emotions, or choices that need transformation.

_____
_____
_____
_____
_____
_____
_____
_____
_____
_____
_____
_____
_____
_____
_____
_____
_____
_____
_____
_____
_____
_____

Review of Week Five

1. Have you been praying / talking to an accountability partner on a regular basis? If you don't have one perhaps you should ask the Lord about finding one for you.

   - Yes

   - No

   - No, but I plan to ask _____ to be a partner.

2. Have you considered finding a disciple to share what you have been learning? Perhaps God wants you to become a prayer mentor to help someone else.

   _____

   _____

   _____

   _____

   _____

   _____

   _____

   _____

   _____

   _____

   _____

   _____

   _____

   _____

3. What revelation have you received from the Lord this past week?

4. What scripture verses have been quickened to you?

_____

_____

5. In what ways has your life changed for the better since you began the Challenge?

_____

_____

_____

_____

_____

_____

_____

_____

6. How have you grown closer to the Lord?

_____

_____

_____

_____

_____

_____

_____

_____

_____

_____

_____

THOUGHT FOR THE WEEK

Only in times of quiet, away from the hustle and bustle of daily life, with nothing and no one to distract us, can Jesus give us His love more fully and more intimately.... Let us be faithful in our quiet times, keeping them holy for Him. —Balilea Schlink

Day Thirty-Six

PRECIOUS AND WEIGHTY THOUGHTS

How precious and weighty also are Your thoughts to me, O God!
How vast is the sum of them! (Psalm 139:17 AMP).

DAILY PRAYER

Every word from God is more priceless than all the treasures in the world. Cherish each nugget the Lord gives you as precious and weighty, of infinite value. Receive, absorb every whisper, word, truth, picture, impression. Don't just think about it, but hold it in your heart, write it down without leaving His presence, and immediately return to Him.

Healing Prayer

Invite the Lord to search all areas of your life. As He heals your heart, allow God to minister to you and give you fresh revelation.

- Pray through roots that have hindered you from hearing God clearly. Forgive God, self, and others.
- Repent for letting revelation pass unnoticed. Ask God to restore precious gems of truth that were lost.

Day Thirty-Seven

GROWTH AND INCREASE

So then neither he who plants is anything, nor he who waters, but God who gives the increase (1 Corinthians 3:7).

DAILY PRAYER

Every revelation from the heart of God to man is full of His love, and its life source is derived from God Himself. When it is planted in the heart, it will grow. How carefully we tend it determines how much it will grow, but it is God who gives the increase. Welcome the presence of God to show you something that He wants you to pay attention to so that it will grow in your life.

_____

_____

_____

_____

_____

_____

_____

_____

_____

_____

_____

_____

_____

_____

HEALING PRAYER

Invite the Lord to search your heart for roots or bad attitudes that may be hindering the increase that He wants to bring into your life.

- Pray through roots that have caused lack of increase.
- Forgive God, self, and others.

Day Thirty-Eight

SEEDS

The kingdom of God is as if a man should scatter seed on the ground, and should sleep by night and rise by day, and the seed should sprout and grow, he himself does not know how. For the earth yields crops by itself: first the blade, then the head, after that the full grain in the head (Mark 4:26-29).

DAILY PRAYER

Welcome every impression, scripture or vision to grow and increase from the place of union and communion. Stay in prayer and the Lord will cause that revelation to grow. Everything that comes from God has life in it, and it will grow if you just let God bring the increase. Dennis and I allow these precious God thoughts to develop and grow, and discover that they grow into sermons, teachings, strategies to help others, and eventually dreams to be fulfilled. Ask the Lord to share a weighty and precious thought with you now, and write it down.

_____

_____

_____

_____

_____

_____

HEALING PRAYER

Allow God to plow up any hard ground in your heart to make it more receptive for revelation to take root and grow.

- Let the Lord search your heart for areas where there is hard ground, thorns (cares of this life), or stony places that have blocked growth.

SECTION 4

DAYS 39-60

FUNCTIONING IN THE SPIRIT

Day Thirty-Nine

RIVERS OF LIVING WATER
IV. FUNCTIONS OF YOUR SPIRIT
Forgiving

[W]hoever drinks of the water that I shall give him will never thirst. But the water that I shall give him will become in him a fountain of water springing up into everlasting life (John 4:14).

He that believeth on me, as the scripture hath said, out of his belly shall flow rivers of living water (John 7:38 KJV).

DAILY PRAYER

There are four primary functions of your human spirit: forgiving, loving, releasing, and receiving. Each one depends on yielding the heart to God, because He is the source of all good things. Forgiveness is the gift Jesus gave us to remove barriers between God and man, and man to man. As you yield and Christ forgives through you, a river of living water flows out from the deepest part of your innermost being, your heart, the seat of your emotions. Freely release rivers of forgiveness in advance to whoever may offend during the day.

Healing Prayer

Allow forgiveness to flow freely to whoever God shows you. You did nothing to earn it, so give as freely as you received.

- Deal with every person and situation that the Lord reveals to you.
- Release forgiveness to God, self, and others.

Day Forty

THE FLOW OF LOVE

You are a fountain [springing up] in a garden, a well of living waters, and flowing streams from Lebanon. [You have called me a garden, she said] Oh, I pray that the ...north wind and the... south wind may blow upon my garden, that its spices may flow out [in abundance for you in whom my soul delights]. Let my beloved come into his garden and eat its choicest fruits (Song of Solomon 4:15-16 AMP).

DAILY PRAYER

You can give to others whatever you have received from God. The whole world needs the forgiveness and the love of God. Allow the love of God to flow out to others during the day.

_____

_____

_____

_____

_____

_____

_____

_____

_____

_____

Healing Prayer

Allow the Lord to show you any areas where you have been blocking the flow of His anointing in your life.

- Release forgiveness to every person that the Lord reveals to you.

Day Forty-One

LIFE AND HEALING

And it shall be that every living thing that moves, wherever the rivers go, will live. There will be a very great multitude of fish, because these waters go there; for they will be healed, and everything will live wherever the river goes (Ezekiel 47:9).

DAILY PRAYER

Practice loving forgiveness again today. Notice that whenever you are releasing love you experience a deep sense of satisfaction. When you allow love to flow out to others who are hurting, you are releasing the compassion of Christ. Multiple times in the Gospels, we read that miracles occurred when the heart of Jesus was moved with compassion. Release forgiveness like a river and wherever it goes forth it brings life.

HEALING PRAYER

If we don't get our way with people, we often react to them as they are inanimate objects depriving us of what we deserve. Whenever we are frustrated or impatient with circumstances, we are really angry at God. He didn't do anything wrong, but the sinful human nature likes the world to revolve around selfish desires and personal convenience. In Matthew 5:21-22, Jesus says, "I'm telling you that anyone who is so much as angry with a brother or sister is guilty of murder."

- Receive forgiveness for judging God, and forgive Him for things that might not go as you wish during the day.
- Release forgiveness in advance to people.

Day Forty-Two

FORGIVE IN ADVANCE

Don't grieve God. Don't break his heart. His Holy Spirit, moving and breathing in you, is the most intimate part of your life, making you fit for himself. Don't take such a gift for granted. Make a clean break with all cutting, backbiting, profane talk. Be gentle with one another, sensitive. Forgive one another as quickly and thoroughly as God in Christ forgave you (Ephesians 4:30-32 MSG).

DAILY PRAYER

Forgive in advance all offenses that will come today. Christ the Forgiver lives in you, and He already knows what will happen. He already paid the price for the sins of the ones who will wound you, disrespect you, and make you angry today. You will please Him so much if you forgive just as He forgave, before it ever even happened.

HEALING PRAYER

Invite the Lord to show you the "little things" which grieve His heart but you yourself overlook.

- Allow God to deal with complaining and ingratitude toward Him.
- Let God wash and cleanse your heart of judgments toward the body of Christ.

Review of Week Six

1. What are the main thoughts that the Lord has been speaking to your heart? List a few of them here.

    _____

    _____

    _____

    _____

    _____

    _____

    _____

    _____

2. What scripture verses had special life to them?

    _____

    _____

    _____

    _____

    _____

    _____

    _____

    _____

3. What theme(s) have you noticed in your emotional healings?

    _____

    _____

    _____

    _____

    _____

_____

_____

4. What changes have you noticed in your life since Day One?

_____

_____

_____

_____

_____

_____

_____

_____

THOUGHT FOR THE WEEK

Because we are the most forgiven people in the world, we should be the most forgiving people in the world. —C. J. MAHANEY[1]

_____

_____

_____

_____

_____

_____

_____

_____

1. Mahaney, C. J. (2002). *Pastoral Leadership for Manhood and Womanhood*, ed. Wayne Grudem and Dennis Rainey, Crossway. 202.

Day Forty-Three

Prepare Your Heart to Forgive in Advance

Then Peter came to [Jesus] and said, "Lord, how often shall my brother sin against me, and I forgive him? Up to seven times?" Jesus said to him, "I do not say to you, up to seven times, but up to seventy times seven (Matthew 18:21)

Daily Prayer

Release forgiveness to those with whom you come in contact with today. Whenever you are tempted to be offended, allow a river of forgiveness to flow out before you respond in any negative way.

Healing Prayer

Love and forgive both friend and foe. Jesus said that we are no better than the unsaved if we only love those who love us. Forty-six percent of all Christians no longer go to church because they were hurt in church. The main reason they isolate themselves is their failure to forgive. Have you allowed the Lord to adjust your attitude toward pastors and church members who have misunderstood you, judged you, wounded, or embarrassed you in the past?

- Welcome the Holy Spirit to go deep into the dark places to set you free from the walls of fear that you hide behind.

Day Forty-Four

River of Grace and Power
Loving

He showed me the river whose waters give life, sparkling like crystal, flowing out from the throne of God and of the Lamb through the middle of the broad way of the city; also, on either side of the river was the tree of life with its twelve varieties of fruit, yielding each month its fresh crop; and the leaves of the tree were for the healing and the restoration of the nations (Revelation 22:1-2).

Daily Prayer

The purpose for your creation and salvation was that you might love God. You have been given the amazing privilege to love the God who is Love. The world was created by love and redeemed by love. And Jesus, the One who died for you, wants you to love Him as a bride loves her bridegroom, forsaking all other loves for her Beloved. Just think. That is all Jesus really wants you to do. And in loving Him above all else, love becomes your motivation and your teacher. Love is so powerful that it breaks through the walls in the hearts of people. Practice going to the supermarket, workplace, or church dinner and emanate loving without words. Many times people will be drawn to come talk to you and not understand why.

_____

_____

_____

_____

_____

_____
_____
_____
_____

HEALING PRAYER

Come before the Lord with gratitude for all that He is doing in your life. Allow the Lord to search the hidden places for hurts, fears, shame, and anger. Allow Him to go deeper still to deal with roots to more subtle forms of anger such as frustration and impatience.

Ask the Lord to heal the hurts and fears in your heart that keep you from knowing His love for you, and prevent you from loving Him as fervently as you desire.

_____
_____
_____
_____
_____
_____
_____
_____
_____
_____
_____
_____
_____
_____
_____
_____

Day Forty-Five

LOVING INTERCESSION

Beloved, let us love one another, for love is of God; and everyone who loves is born of God and knows God (1 John 4:7).

DAILY PRAYER

Let a river of love flow out to family, loved ones, and those that the Lord brings to mind. Love is a powerful spiritual force, and there is no distance in the spirit. If you release love from the belly to a dear friend on the mission field in Africa or India, they can often sense that someone is praying for them. If you are concerned about your child who is away on a trip, your loving intercession is actually releasing divine intervention to work on his or her behalf.

HEALING PRAYER

Trust is the foundation of all relationships, and fear or insecurity in your relationship with God indicates a need for healing in this area. He knows that we cannot change ourselves, so we hide from God and one another. We are all ensnared in our past wounds and sinful nature unless His love sets us free. The walls of childhood become the traps of adulthood.

- Let God go anywhere in your heart and forgive as He leads.
- If you felt any fear or doubt that God would work as you pray, allow God to deal with any root issues of trust.

Day Forty-Six

RIVER OF LOVE

I am my beloved's, And my beloved is mine (Song of Solomon 6:3).

DAILY PRAYER

Yield to God's love toward you, and allow love to flow back to Him. Do you long for more of this great love? If the Lord has placed this desire in your heart, your prayer will surely be answered. Now allow loving intercession to flow out on behalf of others.

HEALING PRAYER

Welcome the Lord to search in all the secret recesses of your heart. Run to His love and His light, and allow Him to expose and cleanse the hidden wounds and toxic attitudes.

- Forgive God, self and others.

Day Forty-Seven

BLESSING

But I say unto you, Love your enemies, bless them that curse you, do good to them that hate you, and pray for them which despitefully use you, and persecute you (Matthew 5:44).

DAILY PRAYER

Allow a river of loving intercession to flow to your loved ones before you open your mouth to say, "Lord, bless them and keep them". Forgive those who have harmed you and the Lord will protect you and then deal with them. Know that God is at work even if you can't see it. In other words, work on you and leave the results in the hands of God. Proverbs 16:7 says, "When a man's ways please the LORD, He makes even his enemies to be at peace with him."

HEALING PRAYER

Release difficult people into the hands of God until you feel peace. When you deal with your own heart, the Lord will deal with those who have been your enemies in His way and His time.

- Release yourself to the Lord, so that you don't try to keep yourself safe, but allow Him to guard you through peace.
- Place your possessions and reputation into God's hands for safekeeping.

Day Forty-Eight

A Fountain Springing Up

Releasing

But he who trusts in the LORD, lovingkindness shall surround him (Psalm 32:10 NASB).

DAILY PRAYER

Release people and circumstances into the hands of God. Trust Him to do what is impossible for you. Release husbands, wives, children, coworkers, friends, and whoever comes to mind. Let an artesian well of living water flow from your heart. Practice this in your prayer time, but continue to trust God all during the day.

HEALING PRAYER

Allow the Lord to go deep in your heart to heal wounds, fine tune your attitudes, set you free, and open wells that need uncapping.

- If you think of a painful memory, remember that you were afraid, but feel numb, receive forgiveness for letting fear guard you, then pray through the issue until you get peace.
- If you have a place where you retreat into yourself when you are afraid, receive forgiveness for the fear and welcome the Lord to flood that area and surround you with His presence.

_____

_____

_____

_____

_____

_____

_____

_____

_____

_____

_____

_____

_____

_____

_____

_____

_____

_____

Day Forty-Nine

LET IT GO

Give all your worries and cares to God, for he cares about you (1 Peter 5:7 NLT).

DAILY PRAYER

Release all the things that weigh you down and cause you anxiety into the hands of God. This applies to circumstances, schedules, demands and expectations. Fretting doesn't cause the answers to come any sooner, it just prevents you from enjoying today.

HEALING PRAYER

Part of the reason for worry and striving is doubting the goodness of God. This was how the serpent tricked Eve in the book of Genesis. He cast suspicion on the character of God and led Eve to believe that the Lord was holding back something good from her.

- Welcome the Lord to search your heart for root issues connected to being suspicious of God's intentions toward you.
- When you have prayed that through, release people and circumstances back into the hands of a loving God.

REVIEW OF WEEK SEVEN

1. What are the main thoughts that the Lord has been speaking to your heart?

_____

_____

_____

_____

_____

2. Write one or two of the scriptures that stand out. Why?

_____

_____

_____

_____

_____

3. What have you released to the Lord this past week?

_____

_____

_____

_____

_____

_____

4. How have you been successful in walking in peace in your daily life? Every baby step of obedience builds spiritual strength so rejoice in even small victories.

_____

_____

_____

_____

_____

_____

_____

_____

THOUGHT FOR THE WEEK

Bridal love for Jesus is nourished and grows when we daily bind ourselves to Him. The dedication of the will leads us into the deepest union of love with Jesus. The true test of bridal love is the willingness to submit wholly to the will of God, even when He frustrates our dearest wishes or we cannot understand what He is doing either in our lives or in the lives of others. To nurture bridal love and to show Jesus that we love Him, we need constantly to practice submitting to His will and wishes.... The time has come for the genuineness of my love to be tested.... I can prove my love for Him by loving His will. —BASILEA SCHLINK[1]

_____

_____

_____

_____

1. Schlink, B. (1969). *My All for Him.* Bloomington, MN: Bethany Press International. 77-78.

Day Fifty

LET GO AND LET GOD

Lean on, trust in, and be confident in the Lord with all your heart and mind and do not rely on your own insight or understanding. In all your ways know, recognize, and acknowledge [divine intimate contact] Him, and He will direct and make straight and plain your paths (Proverbs 3:5-6 AMP).

DAILY PRAYER

You cannot trust God and be stressed at the same time. In the Hebrew, one definition of *trust* is *to make someone your refuge.* When you feel tense, notice how you feel in the belly. It feels tight, not relaxed and open, and the emotion is mild anxiety or worse. That means that you are holding on. When you release a person or circumstance to God, you are not letting go into nothingness, but into the most powerful, trustworthy, and loving hands in the universe.

HEALING PRAYER

Out of your innermost being, through the connection of Christ within, from that place of TRUST let go and let God.

- Release all control of circumstances, deadlines, schedules back into the hand of God.
- Welcome God to search your heart for roots that are interfering with your trust for God today.
- Forgive, release demands, and allow God to fill in areas of need, such as for approval, love, affirmation, security.

Day Fifty-One

WAIT FOR GOD

I waited patiently for the LORD; And He inclined to me, And heard my cry (Psalm 40:1).

DAILY PRAYER

Yield to God's timetable not yours. God is never too early, and He is never too late. Release your schedule into the loving cadence of the Lord.

HEALING PRAYER

If waiting for God to bring promises to pass has been a difficult area in your life, welcome Him to go into the dark places in your heart and heal wounds, but also deal with roots of insecurity and impatience.

- Allow forgiveness to flow to God, self, and others.
- Let go of anything you have been clinging to.

RELEASE DEMANDS AND EXPECTATIONS

They are God's servants, not yours. They are responsible to Him, not to you. Let Him tell them whether they are right or wrong. And God is able to make them do as they should (Romans 14:4 Living Bible).

DAILY PRAYER

Release demands and expectations on people. Release what you want them to do that they are not doing, and what you do not want them to do. Release demands that you put on *yourself*. You belong to God, not you.

Healing Prayer

Continue to welcome God to search your heart for situations where you felt forced to take control, your parents put too much responsibility on you, or it made you feel good to be the rescuer for others. Allow God to go to the root.

- Receive forgiveness, release forgiveness.
- Release demands and expectations on yourself back to God.

Day Fifty-Three

RELEASE YOURSELF TO GOD

[You] are God's servants, not [your own]. [You] are responsible to Him, not to you. Let Him tell [you] whether [you] are right or wrong. And God is able to make [you] do as [you] should (Romans 14:4 LB).

DAILY PRAYER

"God's kingdom come, His will be done (not yours), on earth as it is in heaven." Release demands and expectations back into the capable hands of God. Release yourself to God. "*You* are God's servant not yours. *You* belong to Him and not to *you*. He is able to tell *you* if *you* are right or wrong and to make *you* do as *you* should." Stay in prayer and let the Lord saturate you with this truth.

Healing Prayer

Do you ever feel frustrated with yourself in your Christian life? Have you secretly judged yourself, that maybe you are not spiritual enough, or diligent enough? Those are standards of your own making. God wants you to leave your spiritual progress up to Him.

- Receive forgiveness for living by a man-made standard that is not the standard of the Cross.
- Allow the Lord to heal heart wounds that are contributing to your frustration.

RECEIVE GOD'S CARE
Receiving

*If God gives such attention to the appearance of wildflowers—
most of which are never even seen—don't you think He'll attend
to you, take pride in you, do His best for you? What I'm trying to
do here is to get you to relax, to not be so preoccupied with getting,
so you can respond to God's giving. People who don't know God
and the way He works fuss over these things, but you know both
God and how he works. Steep your life in God-reality, God-ini-
tiative, God-provisions. Don't worry about missing out. You'll
find all your everyday human concerns will be met* (Matthew
6:32-33 MSG).

DAILY PRAYER

Learn to function from your spirit in *receiving*. This is the next loving function of your spirit. In receiving, you are yielding, drinking in, absorbing.
In your prayer time, pay attention to the sense of God's presence and yield
to Him.

Healing Prayer

"Lord, help me cultivate a more implicit trust in you. I choose to live a life of God worship. Please set me free to love you more fully."

- Receive forgiveness for failure to trust.
- Forgive those who failed to be trustworthy in your life.

Day Fifty-Five

BRIDEGROOM KING

I found the one I love. I held him and would not let him go (Song of Solomon 3:4).

The bride . . . looks glorious in her golden gown. In her beautiful robes, she is led to the king, accompanied by her bridesmaids. What a joyful and enthusiastic procession as they enter the king's palace! (Psalm 45:13-15 NLT).

DAILY PRAYER

Jesus wants you to know Him not only as your Savior, or your Provider, He wants to be—your Bridegroom King. As He reveals Himself to you, receive whatever He quickens to you as pure gold.

Healing Prayer

Welcome the Lord to search the inner recesses of your heart for other loves that are competing with His love.

- Receive forgiveness, welcome the work of the cross, lay other loves at His feet, and allow Him to take His place in your heart.

Day Fifty-Six

YOU NEVER WASTE TIME IN GOD'S PRESENCE

But one thing is needed, and Mary has chosen that good part, which will not be taken away from her (Luke 10:42).

DAILY PRAYER

"Come away, My Beloved." You never waste a moment in prayer. You never waste time in the presence of God. Allow whatever the Lord has shown you to be incubated so it can grow.

_____

_____

_____

_____

_____

_____

_____

_____

_____

_____

_____

_____

_____

_____

HEALING PRAYER

Invite the Lord to search your heart for anything hindering the divine romance that He wants to have with you.

- Forgive God, self, and others.

REVIEW OF WEEK EIGHT

1. What are the main thoughts that the Lord has been speaking to your heart?

_____

_____

_____

_____

_____

_____

_____

2. Write one or two of the scriptures that stand out. Why?

_____

_____

_____

_____

_____

_____

_____

3. What difficulties have you overcome?

_____

_____

_____

_____

_____

_____

_____

4. What theme(s) have you noticed in your emotional healings?

_____
_____
_____
_____
_____
_____

5. What are some things that used to bother you, but don't anymore?

_____
_____
_____
_____
_____
_____

THOUGHT FOR THE WEEK

SEVEN BENEFITS OF FORGIVENESS

1. You please God.
2. You feel better inside.
3. You can live in the fruit of the Spirit.
4. You grow emotionally.
5. You make better decisions with peace.
6. You are anointed to be a blessing to others.
7. You have better health.

Motivated by Love

*Christ's love has moved me to such extremes. His love has the first
and last word in everything we do* (2 Corinthians 5:13 MSG).

Daily Prayer

Just as you have welcomed Christ's love for you, now focus on your love
flowing back to Him. Jesus gave Himself completely for you. His love has
been healing your heart and removing barriers so that you can know His
love, and you can return love back to Him. Let this love be the motivation behind all your obedience and service to Him. Focus on Christ within
you. Receive, cherish, absorb, honor, and welcome any word or impression
He gives.

Healing Prayer

Ask the Lord to reveal any personal opinion or preference, no matter how small, that is blocking your flow of love.

- Receive forgiveness, forgive others.
- Release your ideas and desires to God, and ask Him for His ideas and desires.

Day Fifty-Eight

LIVING EPISTLES

Clearly you are an epistle of Christ, ministered by us, written not with ink but by the Spirit of the living God, not on tablets of stone but on tablets of flesh, that is, of the heart (2 Corinthians 3:3).

DAILY PRAYER

When God touches you He leaves an imprint of His nature on your spirit. Allow it to be written on your heart in ever deepening truth.

HEALING PRAYER

Ask the Lord to show you any words or beliefs about yourself which have left a negative imprint on your life. Often these words form part of a false identity, or personality, that blocks the expression of the New Creation.

- Allow the Lord to show you where any false identity came in.
- Forgive whoever said it, including yourself, receive forgiveness for taking it in, renounce it, then ask the Lord to tell you what He says about who you really are.
- Write down what God says to you!

Day Fifty-Nine

REALITY

Write these commandments that I've given you today on your hearts. Get them inside of you and then get them inside your children. Talk about them wherever you are, sitting at home or walking in the street; talk about them from the time you get up in the morning to when you fall into bed at night. Tie them on your hands and foreheads as a reminder; inscribe them on the doorposts of your homes and on your city gates (Deuteronomy 6:9 MSG).

DAILY PRAYER

Whatever God writes on your heart touches your entire being. Even the cells of your physical body are changed by His love. Welcome Him into every organ and system.

Healing Prayer

Welcome the presence of God, Christ the Healer within, to saturate your entire being, every cell of your body, with His reality.

- Ask the Lord to show you any emotional connections to physical ailments with which you may be suffering.
- Pray through forgiveness until you get peace.
- Do not beg for healing, but receive it and welcome the flow of healing anointing from Christ the Healer in you.

Day Sixty

No Barriers

May He grant you out of the rich treasury of His glory to be strengthened and reinforced with mighty power in the inner man by the [Holy] Spirit [Himself indwelling your innermost being and personality]. May Christ through your faith [actually] dwell (settle down, abide, make His permanent home) in your hearts! May you be rooted deep in love and founded securely on love, That you may have the power and be strong to apprehend and grasp with all the saints [God's devoted people, the experience of that love] what is the breadth and length and height and depth [of it]; [That you may really come] to know [practically, through experience for yourselves] the love of Christ, which far surpasses mere knowledge [without experience]; that you may be filled [through all your being] unto all the fullness of God [may have the richest measure of the divine Presence, and become a body wholly filled and flooded with God Himself]! (Ephesians 3:16-19 AMP).

Daily Prayer

Don't let ANYTHING come between what you and the Lord have together. He rejoices over you. Delight in the precious moments that you spend with Him because you are His beloved! Draw near to Him. You have everything you need...*because everything you need is in Him!*

_____
_____
_____
_____
_____
_____
_____

HEALING PRAYER

Allow the Lord to show you any barriers that are keeping you from going deeper in Him. "Lord, I have begun a brand new journey with You, and I am hungry for even more. Lead me into more of your love and glory than I can even imagine!"

- Receive forgiveness for yourself, and forgive God and others.
- Allow forgiveness to flow through barriers or walls of unbelief.
- Receive, absorb, drink in all that God has given to you during the Simple Prayer 60 Day Challenge.

_____
_____
_____
_____
_____
_____
_____
_____
_____
_____

Review of Sixty Days

1. How has the *Simple Prayer Guided Journal* changed your relationship with God?

_____

_____

_____

_____

_____

_____

_____

_____

_____

_____

_____

2. What promises have you received from the Lord?

_____

_____

_____

_____

_____

_____

_____

_____

_____

_____

_____

_____

3. What changes have you noticed in yourself? What changes have other people noticed in you?

_____

_____

_____

_____

_____

_____

_____

_____

_____

_____

4. What are some of the most significant revelations that you have received from the Lord?

_____

_____

_____

_____

_____

_____

_____

_____

_____

_____

_____

I will betroth you to Me forever; yes, I will betroth you to Me in righteousness and justice, in lovingkindness and mercy; I will betroth you to Me in faithfulness, and you shall know the LORD (Hosea 2:19-20).

Notes

About the Authors

Drs. Dennis and Jen Clark minister together as a husband and wife team and are Senior Pastors of Kingdom Life Church in Fort Mill, South Carolina. They are also founders and directors of Full Stature Ministries and TEAM Embassy School. Dennis holds a PhD in Theology and Jen holds a ThD in Theology as well as BS, MS, and EdS degrees in psychology. Visit the authors online at www.forgive123.com

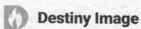

Printed in Great Britain
by Amazon

24808120R00110